SONGS OF INDIA

RENDERED FROM THE

URDU, HINDI, AND PERSIAN

Owing to the antiquity and rarity of this book, certain pages are regrettably absent, and readability is compromised due to the blurring of the original text. If you possess any insights regarding the availability of these missing sections, kindly inform us. Your assistance is crucial in ensuring the completion of this significant work for the benefit of future generations.

SONGS OF INDIA

RENDERED FROM THE

URDU, HINDI, AND PERSIAN

INAYAT KHAN

JESSIE DUNCAN WESTBROOK

GYAN

Published by

GYAN

Gyan Publishing House
5, Ansari Road
Daryaganj, New Delhi-110002
Phone: 011-47034999, 9811692060
E-mail: books@gyanbooks.com

Distribution Network
gyanbooks.com
India, USA, Canada, UK, Australia

ISBN: 978-93-6780-168-0 (PB)

First Published, 1915

2nd Impression 2024

Printed at: Gyan Press, Delhi.

SONGS OF INDIA:
RENDERED FROM THE URDU, HINDI, AND PERSIAN
Author: INAYAT KHAN, JESSIE DUNCAN WESTBROOK

INAYAT KHAN

and his Staff,

The Royal Musicians of Hindustan.

SONGS OF INDIA

RENDERED FROM THE

URDU, HINDI, AND PERSIAN

BY

INAYAT KHAN

AND

JESSIE DUNCAN WESTBROOK

Sufism is the Religious Philosophy of
Love, Harmony and Beauty

LONDON
THE SUFI PUBLISHING SOCIETY, LTD.
100D, ADDISON ROAD, W.
1915

Foreword

As much interest has been roused of late in Indian music it is hoped that the present little volume giving some idea of the words of Indian songs may be found useful.

These songs come from the actual repertory of an Indian singer of to-day, and most of them have been taken down from his dictation as he has learned them—not from books (although many of them are to be found in books), but handed on verbally from singers who were his teachers. Some are the singer's own composition, for often in India, as of old in Europe, bard and musician are one. Most of them are in Urdu and Persian, and are songs of the Sufic tradition. Others are in Hindi, and show how near in thought and inspiration are the poets of the two different languages and creeds. Some are religious songs, sung by devotees at the shrines of Muslim Saints or in Hindu temples; others again are the lighter songs of everyday to be heard in the streets; but all are well-known in India and widely sung. This little collection then aims at giving some suggestion of the intellectual content of the songs which are wedded to that music of dream and reverie which we in the West are now beginning to appreciate.

J. D. W.

Contents

I

To win, O Lord, to Thee
The learned and the wise shall strive in vain,
Useless their knowledge and their skill shall be
Thy presence to attain.

And vain alike the quest
Of those who earthly paths or heavenly choose,
He who the peace of God attaineth best
His very self must lose.

Thee in Thy infinite might
All beings contemplate, and loud and sweet
Through the seven earths and nine heavens high and bright
Thy great Name they repeat.

Unseen, within the heart,
Pervading all, and dwelling by our side,
Close as our self, yet far aloof Thou art,
Remote dost Thou abide.

The idle state of kings
Endures but for a little length of days,
Before Thy gateway till the end of things
The regal music plays.

Before thine eager eyes
Faces like peris', houris' forms have shone,
O Zahir, in their beauty ; now there lies
But dust where they have gone.

From the Urdu of ZAHIR.

II

THOUGH prisoned in this form of dust, my heart
Lives in the Heaven where it hath dwelt before,
And on my lips the self-same tale unfolds
Continued from of yore.

I know not shall the Lord of Beauty deign
To cast a glance upon my waiting face,
But here before his gate my rug is spread,
Here is my dwelling-place.

Thy humble lover to Thy generous board
To crave a drop of wine his cup doth hold,
Knowing the rich and precious store Thou hast,
Hoarded from days of old.

From the Urdu.

III

WHAT happiness were mine beyond all price
  To see thee even for a moment's space,
My life had been a willing sacrifice,
  My soul had bowed before thy worshipped face.

If thou had lived on faith that faithless proved,
  By sweet words fooled, by promises deceived,
Be just and tell me, would'st thou still have loved?
  Still built thy hopes on shadows, still believed?

Thy promises, O Snarer of my heart,
  Had held my faith, could I but put my trust
In life itself, but fickle as thou art
  Life is as frail and all its hopes are dust.

But what is love unless there flame again
  A fire to answer this within my breast?
My heart uneasy tosses in its pain,
  And even thine, unquiet, knows no rest.

From the Urdu of DAGH.

IV

It was not written that I should attain
My heart's desire, and I have yearned in vain.
Did I live longer, what had Fortune willed—
More fruitless pain, more longing unfulfilled.

I lived upon thy promises, yet knew
That they were false—I never held them true;
Thine idle word had I but credited,
The sudden ecstasy had smote me dead.

I knew thee faithless, why should I bewail
Thy promise like thyself—so false and frail?

Here is thine arrow torturing me anew,
Fast in my heart but only half-way through,
I had not known had I been killed outright
This sweet unending pain, this keen delight.

O friends, what is this friendship that you boast?
Where is the kindness that I plead for most?
No one can give me words of sympathy,
Nor for my madness find a remedy.

My cord of life is broken by my grief,
How can I save myself and win relief?
If from the pain of love my heart were free,
Then life itself had been my malady.

Why should I flinch before Death's heavy blow,
That comes but once indeed? Alas, I know
The night of grief wherein I died forlorn
Innumerable times before the morn!

What ignominy is it thus to die
Scoffed at by all! O, in the waves to lie
Deep in the river dead, then none could see
My body or my tomb to mock at me.

Who shall behold her in her beauty dressed?
She stands alone, peerless and loveliest!

From the Urdu of GHALIB.

VII

PIERCING the veil of dawn the Sun looks through,
Then come the morning breezes cool with dew
To call the waking world to work anew.

One to the mosque with pious steps hath sped,
And one within the temple bows his head,
While many rise to toil for daily bread.

I asked my heart "Where doth thy journey lie?"
It weeping said "Like all love's victims I
Must seek the Well-Belovéd till I die."

From the Urdu.

VIII

I HELD the face of the Beloved to be
  The very face of God to bless my sight;
And thus not I alone, but all who read
  The teaching of the holy Saints aright.

Free is the soul to hold what thing it will,
  And many are the paths mankind has trod,
Some take the idol as a clod of clay,
  But we have held our idol to be God.

The learnéd who have cast their lore aside,
  What have they in their newer wisdom seen?
They hold this earth's existence to be naught
  And true existence that which hath not been.

O Friends, this is the wisdom that I teach
  For guidance in this shifting world of dreams,
To see through passing shows the Hidden One,
  And hold as non-existent that which seems.

He who, to the Belovéd's will resigned,
  Gives life, no price demanding, shall possess,
O Zamin, holy joy as those who died,
  Martyrs in Kerbela's dark wilderness.

From the Urdu of ZAMIN.

IX

WITHIN the Tavern walls what joy is there
If the Beloved be not the Cup-bearer?
What joy has love if still the heart remain
Knowing not the supreme delight of pain?
And though the lover has the pride to know
That the world deems him mad, yet he shall go
Unsatisfied indeed unless he gain
This restless torturing joy, this cherished pain.
Love is my Master, and my God as well,
His serf am I; what matter where I dwell
In Kaaba courts, or in the idol's cell?

From the Urdu.

X

THY grace shines everywhere, and Thou art true,
King art Thou, high above all mortal powers,
Thou art the hues and fragrance of the flowers,
And from the nightingale we hear anew
Thy grace shines everywhere, and Thou art true.

Lovely art Thou, and even loveliness
Itself Thou art; that which is manifest
In all the changing universe expressed,
And that behind, which all these shows express.

Death goes and comes obedient to Thy will,
All things are in Thy hands, as Thou hast said,
Thou choosest one to raise from out the dead
And one to die, and one to linger still.

To every mortal hast Thou given his fate,
One is made Shah, another is Amir,
One is an outcast, one is a fakir,
For all hast Thou ordained their world's estate.

One word Thou saidst, and into being grew
The heavens and earth and men and angels all;
Compassionate, before Thy feet I fall!
Save sinful Nussim, who will sing anew
Thy grace shines everywhere, and Thou art true.

From the Urdu of NUSSIM.

XI

O FAITHLESS one, she will not come to me,
    She does not care,
Up to her gates to beat impetuously
    I send my prayer,
But it falls back to me; it does not care.

Death hath a thousand ways to come to me,
    If it should care
To come through her,—killed by her cruelty,
    Caught in her snare,
What joy were mine; but no, Death does not care.

Were the wind kind, then it would come to me,
    —Did it but care,
Bearing upon its pinions tenderly
    Scent of her hair
To make me swoon; indeed, it does not care.

O faithless one, she will not come to me,
Why should she care?
My rival's house stands near invitingly,
Why should she fare
Further upon my road;—she does not care.

From the Urdu.

XII

"ONLY one God there is" the pious say,
  Bowing to Allah who is Lord and King,
But all the weary night and all the day
  "There is but one Belovéd" will I sing,
  Though me the fate of Mansur it might bring.

Around my body at the day of death
  Lay neither spices rare nor attar sweet,
Nor camphor with its purifying breath;
  But seek Her dwelling, and from off its street
  Bring me some dust—it may have touched Her
    feet.

From the Urdu.

XIII

CREATOR of all beings, and Thyself
  The Only Being, Ever-blissful One,
The Source of Peace, Omnipotent and All,
  Govinda Lord, and yet Yashoda's Son.

The Master of the poor, Solace of grief,
  Exalted One before whose feet we bow,
The Gardener of the Jungle, Vasudev,
  The Lord of Vraja, Blissful One art Thou.

From the Hindi.

XIV

BEFORE the righteous soul,
Servant of GOD, even the angels bend,
His lotus feet the long-desiréd goal
Where weary pilgrims find their journey's end
In pardon for their sin.
Thus, as the Saint, GOD comes, and man is healed;
And fortunate that happy one within
Whose heart the Mystic Vision is revealed.

From the Hindi.

XV

HOW hard to draw the water,
For deep the Jumna flowed!
And coming from the river,
The blue and shining river,
And walking by the road
I met upon the road
Krishna, who caught me passing,
And from my lota fell
The silver spilling water,
On my sari the water,
See the wet stains that tell,
My tale to all they tell.

Hindi Folk Song.

XVI

O Love, Love, Love,
See how thy dagger my heart has torn!
To the Jumna I sped,
Shining above
High on my head
My water-pitcher of gleaming gold was borne.

There by the water-side
My soul with his cord of love Lord Krishna drew,
I go and come at his will,
Fast am I tied,
Adoring him still,
My Lord is Girdhar beloved, as the beautiful water blue.

From the Hindi of the PRINCESS MIRABAI.

XVII

HE is my Love, my Girdhar Gopal, mine—
Upon His head there gleams the crown divine,
Within His hand the lotus white He bears,
A shining garland round His neck He wears—
He is my very Lord, and He alone.
Mother and Father, kinsfolk I disown,
They are as naught to me; the world may speak,
Only the presence of the Lord I seek.
They know and scoff; but what is it to me
That they make mock of all my ecstasy?
The creeper of my love has climbed on high
Watered by founts of tears that never dry.
Whate'er befall to me, little reck I,
For Krishna's joyful slave is Mirabai.

From the Hindi of the PRINCESS MIRABAI.

XVIII

Radha's Song to Krishna.

WHEN round my soul the lonely darkness lay,
Then camest thou like the coming of the day;
As comes in radiant dreams the Long-Desired
To the sick heart who, faint with yearning, tired
With seeking, hardly knows for what to pray.

Then changed to joy undreamt my longing sore,
Forgotten was myself, my suffering o'er;
But, as to clasp thee all my soul was moved
Thou vanished utterly, my Well-Beloved;
As waked from dreams, thee I beheld no more.

And then a voice spake, mocking my distress,
"Go purge thy passion of its earthliness;
"From thy sick fancy did the dream arise,
"I am not to be seen by mortal eyes;
"Not mine the lips to kiss—the form to press.

" Formless and unattainable am I."
So said the voice, but I can only cry :—
" Thine eyes still haunt me, and it cannot be :
" Lovelier than any lovely thoughts of thee
" The vision was—it was no fancy's lie."

But, O my love, to calm my bitter pain,
Dispel this maya—come to me again.

From the Hindi.

XIX

HOW did my happy soul at last attain
Knowledge divine to fill its empty days?
I fixed mine eyes upon the Guru's feet,
In loving gaze.

I have engraved his word upon my heart,
Nor let doubt shake my faith, nor trouble bend
My stedfast will; and thus my life has gained
Its destined end.

From the Hindi of NARSINHA CHARYA.

XX

SLOWLY among her maids I see her walk,
Her eyes down-cast, her modest head down-bent
Youthfully, like a lily on its stalk;
Her loveliness her only ornament.
But clouds arise, the shadow of the years
Dewing her gay sari with rain like tears.

From the Hindi of INAYAT KHAN.

XXI

How lovely on the down-cast eyelids drawn
The shade of kohl their lashes to bedeck,
And fair as youth itself and white as dawn
The pearls that shine upon her maiden neck!
All other maids admiring shall behold,
Her bracelets fashioned from the purest gold.

From the Hindi of INAYAT KHAN.

XXII

MIGHTY thy power, O Mohan, Heart-compeller,
  In changing aspects known and manifest,
Thou as a man or as a woman comest,
  In earthly form of child or mother dressed.

Praise be to Thee, O Maker and Unmaker,
  Creator and Destroyer; let my mind
Be lost in Thee, that everywhere and ever,
  Thy holy vision shall Inayat find.

From the Hindi of INAYAT KHAN.

XXIII

O SAVE me from the ocean of this life,
This turbulent sea,
And liberate my spirit from its strife;
False is the world, and fleeting are its loves,
Then why to me
Should it keep faith, when it deceitful proves
To all its lovers:—I but share their fate.

Thy love is true and in Thy name we trust,
Most Merciful and Most Compassionate,
Destroy our sorrow, lift us from the dust.

From the Hindi of INAYAT KHAN.

XXIV

No more can pain or sorrow torture me.
  I, the fakir, dwell in a sphere of joy
That circles round my soul in ecstasy,
  Ease hath no lure for me, pain no annoy.

This world's bazar is but a puppet-show
  That plays its coloured pageant for a night,
Its figures act their part and come and go
  And disappear before the morning's light.

The vision of this transitory world
  Is like a children's playground, with a game
Played ever day and night, till it is whirled
  Down to the nothingness from whence it came.

O blesséd be the Holy Name of God!
  I sought Thy gate and now my soul is free.
Where are the Kaaba courts that once I trod
  Where is the shrine of my idolatry?

Beside Thy wine-press all my life has passed,
  The vision of the Guru held me long,
To Brahma did my soul attain at last,
  And lost itself in rapture and in song.

From the Hindi of INAYAT KHAN.

XXV

PRAISE be to thee, O Sayyid and O Leader,
  Of Mecca and Medina Lord thou art,
Before thy many names the soul pays homage
  And yearns for sacrifice the humble heart.

Thy shining vision holds my soul in bondage,
  My heart unto thy loveliness I yield
Made captive by thy many-sided beauty
  In all its aspects variously revealed.

O fortunate the Land that was thy birth-place,
  Happy Arabia to be thus blest,
For in thy tongue to us Koran was given,
  God's message to the world made manifest.

Since thou art there the roses of Medina
  More fresh and green in fragrant beauty spring,
Partaking of thy youth and of thy sweetness,
  This is the tale the passing angels bring.

If I might be the dog that meekly crouches
  Content to wait thy will before thy gate,
How blest were I; but I am all unworthy,
  Too humble for a fate so fortunate.

How high thou art above the sons of Adam,
  Incomparable in thy mightiness,
Greater than earth, higher than man or angel,
  More than my feeble halting words express.

My lips are parched and dry with weary longing,
  Thou art the draught of immortality;
O let me slake the thirst that burns within me;
  Before I die be merciful to me!

O cast on me thine eyes, Only-Belovéd,
  Pride of the Koreish, Friend compassionate,
My Master and my soul's desired Physician,
  O heal thou Kudsi, kneeling at thy gate.

From the Persian of KUDSI.

XXVI

BEWARE! the same Beguiler to deceive
Comes as before; He hides behind His sleeve
The same familiar features. He hath made
This show of earth and in it He hath played
His many parts, and still He comes to see—
Witness and Author of its pageantry.
He in the garden as the opening rose
That gilds the spring in all His beauty glows,
And, as the bulbul, in the autumn grieves
Over the rose's quickly withering leaves.
From many mirrors His reflection gleams
Yet brighter He than all the mirrors beams,
Dimming their light. His was the voice that cried
As Mansur's "I am God!" and, crucified,
He died as Mansur, martyred in his pain;
And yet it was His voice that did ordain
The martyrdom.

To Kudsi, the fakir,
Pondering life and death, He doth appear
Sometimes a slave who pines in misery,
Or as a liberator cometh He
To set Himself, Who is the captive, free.

From the Persian of KUDSI.

XXVII

THE sweetest songs of love the bulbul knows,
  His pain and ecstasy by thee were taught,
The colour and the fragrance of the rose,
  Its delicate beauty—all from thee were caught.

I know no more the place that once was mine,
  Forgotten is the country of my birth,
For me the gardens of Medina shine
  Fairest and most desiréd spot on earth.

Bear humble Jami's greeting from afar,
  For in his heart sorrow and longing stir,
Salute for him the Dargah and Durbar
  Of high Medina's holy Messenger.

From the Persian of JAMI.

XXVIII

ON me your cold and critical eyes are turned
O Orthodox,
I take my Saki by the hand and mock you—what
do I care?
For I am a sinful guest who tarries a day or two
in this world,
And lightly through it I fare.

In the midst of the feast and the revel the sultan
of sinners am I,
In my little house of a Sufi with my Lover I
take my delight,
For I am a sinful guest who tarries a day or two
in this world,
Go—ask for me not to-night!

This cloak of my mortal existence a thousand times
have I pawned,
Extravagant is my soul that barters its honour
for wine,
Mocked at and drunken within the bazar no mantle
of virtue I own,
No turban of piety mine.

A lover of no account, idle and crazy am I,
Whether Muslim or Kafir I know not, and what
do I care,
For I am a sinful guest who tarries a day or two
in this world,
And lightly through it I fare.

Dervish Song, from the Persian of HAFIZ.

XXIX

If the beloved face thou canst not see,
  Within thy heart still cherish the desire;
And if her love she will not grant to thee,
    In thy love never tire.

Although her face be hidden from thy sight,
  Within the sanctuary of thy heart
Still keep her image for thine own delight,
    Hidden, apart.

If the unsympathetic stars still turn
  Unheeding, unpropitious to your prayer,
Life's space is but two days—why should you burn?
    Why should you care?

And if the Keeper of the Garden close
  Before your face the inexorable gate,
O linger yet, the perfume of the rose
  Will float to you and find you as you wait
    Not all disconsolate.

From the Persian of the PRINCESS ZEB-UN-NISSA.

XXX

No learning have I but Love's fantasy ;
The bulbul woos the rose thus cunningly,
He learnt his sorrow and his song from me.

The moth that loves the flame thus ardently,
And, burnt to ashes, dies in ecstasy,
One with his love—he learnt his part from me.

* * * *

O breaking heart, that sheds such tears of blood,
Have pity on mine eyes, for they are tired,
So long have they outpoured a bitter flood.
O sleep my weary eyes, the Long Desired
Will come to you and staunch your burning streams
And bring you comfort in the land of dreams.

* * * *

At every dawn I say—
If not to-day
My joy will come to me to-morrow;
And, hoping for delight,
Dawn becomes night.
And thus, deceived, I find unto my sorrow
At last
That, hoping for to-morrow,
My life has passed.

* * * *

To buy this pain so deep and exquisite
A thousand lives were cheap enough to give;
How can I ever have enough of it,
And if I taste it not, how can I live?

* * * *

My life is like a treasure I have spent,
The ashes of a long-extinguished fire;
I sit with sorrow lonely and repent,
And shed the tears of unfulfilled desire.

* * * *

My heart is happy when in secret wise
It dwells upon the memory of thy grace;
But how can I content my longing eyes
That ask insatiably to see thy face?

*   *   *   *

Fame is not mine, nor all the gorgeous things
That make the splendour and the state of kings:
What matters it;—the crown of life have I,
That love of beauty which is ecstasy.

*   *   *   *

Even as the Zem-Zem well,
Stopped for a time, o'erflows to find relief,
So in my heart love's eager fountains swell,
Bursting the iron prison of my grief.

*   *   *   *

Such bitter joy from my heart's wounds I gain
I bind them not but cherish them indeed;
For when they heal I miss my rapturous pain,
And so I tear them till again they bleed.

*   *   *   *

How can I reach your house, beloved Friend?
  Long is the way I came,
The path is dark, I cannot see the end,
  My horse has fallen lame,
And when I look into my heart, dear Friend,
I cannot find the end.

*   *   *   *

The pages of my book of life in vain
I turn, for only wasted days I find,
As though across my mortal path had lain
The sum of all the sorrows of mankind.

From the Persian of the PRINCESS ZEB-UN-NISSA.

Glossary

Amir	=	rich.
Brahma	=	God in aspect of Creator, in Hinduism.
Bulbul	=	nightingale.
Dargah	=	shrine.
Durbar	=	assembly.
Fakir	=	ascetic, in Islam.
Girdhar, Gopal, Govinda	=	names of Krishna.
Guru	=	spiritual teacher, in Hinduism.
Houri	=	nymph of Heaven.
Jumna	=	Yamuna, sacred river of Hindustan.
Kaaba	=	central shrine of Islam, at Mecca.
Kafir	=	unbeliever.
Kerbela	=	wilderness in Arabia: scene of the martyrdom of Hassan and Husain, grandsons of the Prophet.
Khusru	=	Cyrus, King of Persia in VIth century A.D.
Kohl	=	collyrium, used as cosmetic for the eyes.
Koran	=	sacred Book of Islam.
Koreish	=	Arab tribe to which the Prophet belonged.

Krishna	=	God, in aspect of the Beloved, in Hinduism.
Lota	=	water-pot.
Mansur	=	a Persian Saint of IXth century crucified at Baghdad for declaring he was God.
Maya	=	illusion.
Mecca Medina	=	Holy cities of the Muslims, in Arabia: birth-place and burial-place, respectively, of the Prophet.
Mohan	=	Heart-compeller, name of Krishna.
Muslim	=	or Musulman: one believing in Allah alone.
Peri	=	fairy.
Radha	=	in Hinduism, female type of the human soul as the lover of Krishna.
Saki	=	wine-giver.
Sari	=	Indian woman's dress.
Sayyid	=	Leader: name taken by descendants of the Prophet.
Shah	=	ruler.
Sufi	=	mystic of Islam, and also of other creeds.
Suleiman	=	Solomon, King of the Jews.
Vasudeva	=	name of Krishna.
Vraja	=	holy country of Hinduism, around the birth-place of Krishna.
Yashoda	=	Mother of Krishna.
Zem-Zem	=	holy well at Mecca.

Women's Printing Society, Ltd., Brick Street, Piccadilly.